Design of a Woman

Design of a Woman

JAMES R. MITCHELL

Design of a Woman
by James R. Mitchell

Cover Design by Atinad Designs.

© Copyright 2012

SAINT PAUL PRESS, DALLAS, TEXAS

First Printing, 2012

The name SAINT PAUL PRESS and its logo are registered as a trademark in the U.S. patent office.

ISBN-10: 0615874673
ISBN-13: 9780615874678

Printed in the U.S.A.

Tribute

This book is a tribute to Carolyn (whom I affectionately call "Sam's daughter"), my wife of eighteen wonderful years. She has always been a very smart, remarkable individual. Carolyn has always been very kind to me. She has shown the kindness that most men would use or consider to be weakness. I have always considered her opinions and appreciated her aspirations. She is also an excellent homemaker. I am not writing this because I have agreed with everything my wife has said or done because she is a woman and I am a man. We have learned to be reasonable with each other and to consider each other's ideas and opinions. I have always treated her as though she were the weaker sex, however, she is not weaker than I. The one thing I know about her is that she knows who she is, she knows her value, she knows her opinions count, yet, she is humble and giving.

After reading this book, it is my desire that Carolyn and the rest of the world will know that women are not weaker than men; they just have different strengths. Women have things that men do not have, and vice-versa. This does not equate to one being weaker than the other. I always treat my wife with the same respect that I showed or rendered to my mother. Showing this type of respect for your wife will help men to understand and consider that their mother is the reason for their very existence. So to Carolyn, my help meet, a blessed, virtuous woman, and my bride, I write this book in your honor.

Contents

To The Reader

My hope is that the information contained in this book, coming from a male perspective, will provide a vehicle that will enable both sexes to better understand who they really are. This information is especially for women who do not quite understand who they are, and for men who are supposed to be the leaders in the world, but who have lost touch with the true meaning of leadership.

I hope that the men who come in contact with the information contained in this book would find a dictionary and look up the definition of "leadership" and "domination." After having done this, it is my desire that men will try to get in their proper position in life. Women were made for a special purpose: First, as a help meet, and second, to bear children. I am writing about "human life," and the woman whom God designed to create all mankind.

Acknowledgements

I'd like to thank my wife, Carolyn, for many years of happiness. I also thank her for having the patience to wait on me as she observed me talking to people at various times. Periodically, she would make statements like, "You are always talking to people." Little did she realize, I was gathering information to be included in this book that I have dedicated to her. We made certain agreements before we were married. Those agreements are still in place today. Couples should always consider each other's feelings. They should always respect each other.

I studied the "Design of a Woman" a few years before I met my wife. She had no idea I did that study; she just thought I was a very nice guy. She had mixed emotions about what some people who knew of my past were saying about me. Some of these things came from people she knew to be close associates. This would have been a turn off for some people. However, she refused to listen to them and made her own assessment about the "new man" she met. She said she would judge me on her own. She noticed how I treated her. I was always a gentleman. She also realized I always took the time to help care for her elderly parents. We both took great care of the children we both had before we were married. This made her notice that we both had a sense of family.

Before writing this book, I built her the home of her dreams. This acknowledgement adds more fire to the already fiery flame of great love we share with each other. The greatest thing you will ever learn is to love and be loved in return.

We would like to thank all of our children for believing in both of us. I want to thank all of our brothers and sisters for recognizing that our marriage is the kind of marriage that is usually made up in dreams but not in "real life." This was possible because I realized that women are our equal, and they should be treated that way.

Preface

Several years ago, I became very interested in trying to better understand the relationship between men and women. I started to read books written by different authors. All of the material I read pointed to man becoming the "leader in this universe." As I started to put all of the main issues together, I found that man was not living according to the biblical mandate as to his position in the universe. The Scriptures have a completely different view of man and woman than the world has. I was both amazed and disappointed to find that man's thinking about the plan and design of a woman is very, very far from God's plan and design of a woman. This book was born out of trying to find a way to have the man and woman respond to each other the way that God intended for them to respond and treat each other.

First and foremost, the decision to write about the "design of a woman" became a passion. I have lived in the United States for more than seventy years. During the last ten years or more, I have traveled to many foreign countries. During my visits to these other countries, I found that in many of these countries women were treated as second class citizens.

The women in these foreign countries are raised to have the utmost respect for men. I also noticed that the men in these foreign countries are far more dominant towards women than most of the men in America. I was reared to see women the same way society sees women—as second class citizens. I did not change my views until I became a "Legal Christian." My definition of a "Legal Christian" is a person who has studied the Word of God and gained wisdom, knowledge and understanding in the process. When you understand that you are not only made in His image but that "You are His image," you will understand this book as well. God is not in the earth's realm in the physical. He is here in the spirit of man and woman. When you better understand who you are, then and only then, can you move into the arena of understanding what God's Word says about the woman.

CHAPTER ONE

The Beginning

In the beginning, God made man from the dust of the earth. He was then given the right to be the "leader" in the earth. Then God gave the man someone to help him to maintain the earth, which was a beautiful place to live and to fulfill the statement, "On earth as it is in Heaven." The woman was made by taking something from God's earlier creation and given special details as God showed off His creativity. The woman has the ability to bring both sexes into the earth realm. God did not give this privilege to man but only to woman. This shows that God made her very special just for the man. This was not done so that he would exploit the woman. Men seem to think that because women think differently from them that they are not as smart as they are. This is what you call being misinformed. This kind of thinking causes difficulty in relationships. The woman has been given talents that equal anything that man has.

Since man has not understood the order that God established when He made the man the "leader" of the household, man evidently thought that God was saying that he could lead as many women astray as possible. God made man the leader not a dominator. A real leader leads people into things of structure and not domination. Man has not fully come to understand how blessed he is to have someone to help him meet the many, many challenges in today's world. The man wants the woman to be perfect about everything, yet, he is not perfect. Man wanted God to give him a perfect help meet that would be by his side as a weaker person. Man cannot fathom the idea that God gave him a help meet that is equal to him. Man is saying until this day, "This could not be possible." Man really wants a help meet that is not equal to him so he can be King of his castle. He does not realize, nor does he understand, that he will be recognized as the King of the castle if he follows God's design.

This line of thinking causes a struggle between the woman and the man and the desire of the woman who decided that she wanted to be more in charge of her day-to-day activities. When man and woman started out in the Garden of Eden the woman was happy and the man was happy. Then sin was introduced to them. They were sentenced to a life of labor (Genesis 3:16-19). The journey has been long; the woman has walked in the shadow of man for years and years. She has given birth to children and also been his help meet (Genesis 3:16). They have enjoyed each other throughout the years. In the beginning, the man was the main breadwinner (Genesis 3:19). The man went out to hunt and the woman took care of the house and the children. I feel that the beginning was just great for they relied on each other. They stayed in close contact with each other. This type of family life with the woman and man being dependent on each other must have been great. When there is a dependency factor between women and men, they have a greater sense of satisfaction when they start a family together. The family has existed until this present day.

In most of the foreign countries that I have visited, the women and men alike, seem to hold family life in very high esteem. The men, however, in all of the countries I have visited, seem to think that God has elevated him higher than the woman since he was appointed to be the "leader." Since the woman's assignment was to bear children, the man has mistaken this to equate to the level of him being superior to the woman. This kind of thinking has caused the woman to fight for rights that she was already born to have. My Bible states, "That we all stand in the same place" (Ecclesiastes 3:20). The Bible also states, "That you should not think more highly of one's self than you ought to" (Romans 12:3). Man was assigned a position in life; the woman was also assigned to do certain things based on God's Order of His design in creating man and woman. There is nothing in the Bible that states that because you are a woman you cannot do jobs or things that have been assigned by a man for men. The Bible states, "I can do all things through Christ that strengthens me" (Philippians 4:13).

God is not into gender. The things that are listed in the Bible are for the most part written for both man and woman. The Bible states, "That the man and woman must submit themselves one to another in the fear of God" (Ephesians 5:21). The man has taken things out of the spiritual realm and interpreted them wrongly by bringing them into the "Sense Ruled Realm."

The woman and the man have survived under adverse conditions during the early years of life on earth. The woman helped with many different tasks. The woman helped the man do his work in the fields and many other things that needed to be taken care of in the man's absence. The idea that the woman cannot do things that were started by men is wrong.

I was reared on a farm in Moyock, North Carolina, and have visited farms that almost were run entirely by women. Two hundred years ago during the Slavery period in America, women were at the mercy of the slave master. According to information written in history books regarding things that the woman had to endure during this period, the woman with children and no husband had to do everything for her family. She had to endure the things associated with slaves the same as the man. Women have always done work that some people consider man's work. This type of thinking is in the minds of many men today. I cannot begin to imagine how much strength the woman had. She was and has endured the treatment of the slave master and the man. This indicates that the woman is much stronger than she realizes. The woman has been treated as being less than the man. The man has continued this way of thinking that the woman is not equal to him. Man has not fully understood the order of God. Paul made the statement that, "All men are created equal," this means that all mankind (women and men) are created equal. The reason for man making this error is that many have distorted things that God set in order. Yet, it is very clear, God created the man first then He made the woman from man.

This would indicate that the woman was created out of man. Man was created with the woman in him. God created and designed the woman. There is nothing I have read in the Bible that states that the woman is not equal to the man. During the first two hundred years the woman was mostly domesticated. Men were busy dealing with the struggles of trying to keep the family together. The man at that time worked from sun up to sun down. This was the custom for many, many years. I can remember my father telling me about how people survived in the year of 1910. This was more than one hundred years ago. My Father told me, "Men worked long hours each day. They were off for a half of day on Saturday to go to the Market for the family." While the man was working these long hours, the woman had to take care of the children, cut wood, feed the live stock, cook, wash, draw water from the well and clean the yard. She also sewed clothes and worked in the field. The woman also worked part-time for her husband's employer. Most of the families did not own homes the way that people own homes today. Whenever your employer needed the children and the wife to work, the family had no choice because the boss usually owned their home. The house that the family lived in was based on all of the duties that were assigned to the woman. She has proven through the years that she is capable of handling several tasks at the same time.

If someone is unequal he is perceived to have lesser abilities. So this is a myth, since women take on more tasks than men. With all of these tasks associated with the woman for years and years, there is no reason for her to be considered unequal. I am very much in disagreement with this assessment of inequality for women. I have always made myself available to men of other persuasions, to criticize, to discuss our views and feelings in private or in a public arena about the women in their lives.

I have a real problem with any religion that thinks or teaches that the woman is not equal to man. The Church has failed to recognize that women are equal to men.

One other point that I would like to expound upon is the struggle for equality in a world of "Tongue talking, Bible toting, Bible Reading Christian men." These men did not design the woman, neither did they have anything to do with the creation of this world or the world to come. Man has failed miserably in holding on to his leadership position designed by God. Let's remember that this was designed by the Creator according to the Scriptures and it states that, God does not make mistakes. When you take into account this Scripture, I cannot imagine anyone not coming to understand that God is a God of order. He has created man and woman to complement each other. The word complement means that you complete each other. Think about the words "help meet." That means equal not less. My question is, "Are men now following what God is trying to show and tell them?" The answer is, "No." During the years of slavery the women of the world suffered at the hands of men. The men treated women who were free and the women who were slaves the same way, which was to say that man was greater than woman.

When the woman and the man were released from slavery, the Church that was run by men reading and studying the same Bible that we have today, practiced the same custom of unequal treatment of women. All of the people living in the 17th, 18th and 19th century have, for the most part, been privileged to get a better understanding of how God and the Bible relates to the people. Man, until this present day, has not rendered to God all the things that belong to God. Man has been busy working with the wars and all of the new inventions and factories. The woman started to take on additional roles in life. For example, women began to become business women and started businesses, with many men being killed in war, this caused a shortage of men in the factories, so the women began to take those jobs over and that was truly unheard of during this era. The jobs were done by women; this was the start of changing things that were formally geared to be done by men instead of women. The war created jobs for women which were formally held by men. The women proved that they could do the job and also maintain the family. This type of change did not set very well with macho men, most of whom did not want their wives to work outside of the home. They preferred that their wives be domestic women. This attitude of men towards their wives has somewhat continued until this present time.

When the change began there were many advantages and disadvantages as well. Women who were not married had the opportunity to have what was at that time labeled a man's job. This enabled her to have a job that would put her in a better situation to be the sole breadwinner for her household. During this era, payroll was usually based upon one's gender, and women received less than men. Now, as the family moved into the 19th century, this century changed the ways that women, and the family made a break from the traditional family life as well. In fact, more and more women were both mothers and fulltime workers. This caused both parents to be working which played a very important role in the standard of living for larger families. Yet, the woman and the man had a very difficult time adjusting to this change.

I actually was reared in this era during the 1940's. I can speak on this time in my life because it was always discussed by the men. I used to hear the conversations of men and they did not like many of these changes that were going on in the workplace. The woman was sometimes earning nearly as much as they were. I also discovered that men had problems trying to control the woman once they were earning their own money. He noticed that he had no problem controlling the woman as long as she had only the money that he brought home from work at the end of the week. Now, he became keenly aware that the woman or women were becoming very independent. Man felt threatened that they were no longer in control. This independency was attained by the woman earning her own money. Even when the woman was working, the man maintained control of the woman's finances. I remember my mother and many other women who gave their entire checks to the men after they had worked. The man, for the most part, controlled almost everything that the woman did. The women who were widowed or single with children were able to attain just as much for themselves or their family as the men did.

Men who owned brothels, clubs, and drive-in restaurants where you could be served by women wearing short skirts and roller skates were frequented mostly by men who enjoyed watching scantily dressed woman working and catering to them. However, they did not want their woman to work. This was the way that men led women to think that she evidently was designed to be this kind of woman, dressed in this way, and this idea has not changed but has escalated to where it is today. The men who were happily married did not let their wives or children work at these types of places, yet they themselves visited these places "on the regular."

Men, throughout the years, have failed to embrace their leadership role which God has bestowed on them. The man, according to God's design, is the leader of the family. According to the meaning of the Word of God, the leader would be the one to protect the people that were affected by his leadership. When you are to protect the people who are looking to you for leadership this assignment entails that you do all of the decent things such as not leading them into danger or into places of ill repute. Leaders are not supposed to abuse, beat or treat their families in any unfair manner. Man has never fully understood what the word "leadership" means when it comes to the design of life here on the earth. Man has held on to his convictions relative to the woman until this present time.

Some of the laws and statutes set by man relative to the woman have been relaxed a bit. The laws should be written with the woman in mind. This would not take anything from the man's position in life. Man has not taken this step because he is unwilling to accept or acknowledge that the woman is equal to him. As you read this, perhaps you would think from the beginning of time until this present time that men have not come to understand that the woman is his equal and that men and women are equal. This way of thinking and behaving has caused havoc in society, not to take into account countless families that have been torn apart because of the continuous abuse of women. This abuse is based on two or three main things related to the man's mentality. Men have a big problem understanding why God made man a certain way and why God made the woman a certain way. The reason is very simple. Men and women were designed to be helpers to each other. When a man accepts the woman for who she was designed to be, the problems will be solved forever and ever in their relationship and life.

CHAPTER TWO

Amazing Design

This question is posed to every man and woman: "What is the real problem between you?" The year is 2012; it is the time for all to come to a complete understanding of who the woman really is. This is the year of completion. I am writing this book in a very timely manner. Man has not allowed the woman to be and live according to the way that God designed the human race.

God designed all humans to be equal. They were designed to have different positions, yet be equal human beings. These unequal thoughts should be erased now and forever from our minds. This should have never taken place in the first place. In the beginning of creation, man and woman were very marvelous beings.

God made the man first then He tweaked man and made woman. When you add something you cannot make it less than what it was made out of because the ingredients are the same going in to both parts. God made man then he added "wo" to man and it became "woman." In my opinion, this sounds like God added something. This was done so that man would always have someone to take care of. God wanted man to love her, respect her, and to consider her as an equal.

When God decided to make man, He put the things necessary to fulfill his duties in the earth realm inside of him. Then God looked at what He had created and decided that He needed to add to, or, to put it this way, God decided to take the man that He had made and add woman. Adam had all of this in him. God decided that Adam needed a help meet in the earthly realm; with this help meet man would be able to replenish the earth. All human life that entered the earth would be through the woman God had created. This means that the woman is to be treated in the manner in which God created her to be treated. She is a very special human. Let's take a direct look at this issue. God did not give this assignment to Adam; God gave this assignment to Eve. Adam did not do very well when he had an assignment from God. In fact, Adam failed at his assignment, yet he and all of mankind have blamed the woman for his weakness. Men following Adam have continued in this state up until the writing of this book. While continuing in this state, man has tried to use the woman's mistake in the Garden of Eden to reduce her position in the world. Adam and Eve both made mistakes, but the order was given to man not to eat of the fruit. Yet, Eve was blamed for the mistake and women to this day are still treated as the one who failed man.

The makeup of the woman was designed to be different from the man. They were both designed to be individuals, and this would have had to have been part of the plan of God since everyone does not really want to be married. If the woman or the man were not designed as individuals they would have a very difficult time not having a mate. They were designed with the ability to make several choices. You must have strong considerations for her feelings as well. However, many men become inferior. I think God stepped His making of woman up a notch. Based on the women that I have encountered in my life time including my mother, Annie, I have found some things in the woman which are much greater than in the man. Man should not think of himself more highly than he really is, and this is a biblical statement. Man thinks of himself more highly because he was appointed to be the leader of the family. Remember the leader uses the same bathrooms as the people they are in charge of, they eat the same food, they attend the same schools, and they drive the same cars. They study from the same Bible. Now, can you choose the one that is inferior to the other? When you choose please choose wisely. When you look at the man and woman from God's point of view, you can see that they are both in the same place with different responsibilities. Women are designed to be women and men were designed to be men! God has no respect of person according to His word. This truly indicates that the woman was made to be man's equal. God made woman for man to have someone to love and care for. Man has never considered woman as being equal to him.

To the woman I say, "You are this remarkable being that was carefully designed to be free in a world supposedly led by man!" This was the beginning of a well planned relationship for man and woman who started out in the Garden of Eden and shortly afterwards were removed from that kind of life. After Adam and Eve left the Garden of Eden, they moved into the present earth's realm as we are today. They were to mate and begin the way of life as we enjoy it today. In the beginning, the man would go out and work while the woman would take care of the cooking and the cleaning. In looking at the amazing design of women, one can see that she was designed to bear children. She has endured the hardships of childbirth from the very beginning of time until this present day. With this thought in mind, you can truly understand the amazing design of a woman. The woman has been treated sort of like a second class citizen with the full privilege of delivering all human life into this earthly realm. This was an awesome responsibility bestowed on the woman. After being recognized as this amazing individual, my question is, How can man not realize what the Creator had in mind? The Bible states that, "To whom much is given, much is required." God, the Creator, has shown to the world that He designed the woman for a very special purpose. However, for some unknown reason, man has failed to fully consider the amazing design of the woman which God gave unto him. Based on how men view the woman she sometimes lets fear of judgment get in the way of expressing who she really is.

To the women, I want to say these words, "You can control what happens to you! You can control your attitude towards what happens to you! In so doing, you will be taking control and mastering change in your life rather than allowing it to master you!" Women should always be responsible! Do your own due diligence before responding to any leader. The reasons are very apparent. The leader, (as designed by God), has so manipulated you over the years. You have lost sight of how amazing you really are! It is time for this amazing person that you actually are to start noticing "Herself," and acknowledging who she really is. You, as a woman, must always keep in mind that you are a lady with value like an antique car. The sprint to the finish line must be done while maintaining a positive mental attitude which will give you the ability to think through to the end of a situation. Women, ask yourself, "What was God's design for me?" "What is my value?" Women, act like you are valuable, demand respect and honor your God!

Under the hand of a man a woman has endured hardships and difficulties. Her most difficult task has been trying to please man. At the same time, she has grown stronger under pressure; now she is this amazing diamond. I would hope that the women who read this book would research how and what it takes to be made into a diamond. Women, you have two diamonds: one is made of roughness and the other one is pure. Which diamond are you?

Maybe this amazing design is far too advanced for man to fully comprehend, or to accept this design as being equal to him. The Bible states very clearly that, "We all stand in the same place and He has no respect of person." This says that God considers everyone the same. The Christian man should be the first to realize the error of his ways. It is my desire that this book will prompt him to take his religion to the proper place. Christians who have read the Bible should know how amazing God is. It is time for a break through! It's time for a twenty-first century breakthrough! This should be exciting news for the amazing women who have unanswered questions such as, "What do men have that I don't have?" The answer to that is, "Nothing." The only thing that men have over the woman is that this has become a pattern or habit. Patterns are very difficult to deal with and to break. Many things that are done out of a habit are not always malicious. This amazing woman must take immediate action by taking responsibility in having allowed the man to take this situation to the level that it is. This amazing woman has had the ability and the power to change the way they have been treated by men for as long as they have been created.

Now that you have been pressured into a diamond, this indicates that you are more than ready to move fully into mainstream America. The American man will be the first to come out and discuss sections of this book. I hope he keeps in mind that, "Diamonds are a girl's best friend!" This will cause him some embarrassment when he tries to talk concerning these amazing diamond women. Now is the time for women to overcome all the limiting obstacles and annoying barriers. This information will and should empower women to reprogram their brain. The woman has been brainwashed for years and years. The woman has always treated the man with loving kindness down through the years. Armed with the information in this book, the woman should not think so much about where she stands presently but more about the direction she will be moving into in the very near future.

Today, you know or should know more than you did at this time yesterday. Today you are one day closer to the "Amazing Woman" you were created to be. My goal, is to ensure today, you have more experience and more wisdom than you did before reading this book. You are more amazing today than you have ever been before! Do not ignore the information being offered to you. "We suffer for a lack of knowledge." Make full use of this information. Now that you have become more, it is time for you to do more. As of now, you have and have had what it takes to put more effort into achieving your full entitlements as a woman. The tools and opportunities available to you have increased. Now, you should use them to achieve the results necessary to receive your full right. Listen, women! Do not wait for next week nor say to yourself, "In a couple of days." I say to you, right now is the time. Today is truly golden and you have what it takes to make your life shine more brightly.

Women, you really know that you can do it. You also need to realize that you are not doing anything on your own. I believe the woman has always been somewhat plugged into the "power of the Spirit." Being plugged into the "power of the Spirit," is not all that is needed to correct the things that are continually keeping women as the second class citizens they are perceived to be. There are some missing ingredients in this amazing woman's lifestyle. She has to change things in her lifestyle in order to change the way women are treated in the world today. One of the most important changes that has to take place is in the minds of these amazing women. Women, you are what you think. You cannot move very fast with the mentality that what you say is not important. This type of thinking has been going on for years. Taking this into consideration, you must change your thinking. You must think you are this amazing woman who you were designed to be from the beginning. Remember that you were born a diamond. So from day one you were a diamond, designed by God. You were created in His image and all He made was beautiful.

I really have a very strong desire to help this amazing woman. I want to help men and women share the knowledge God has given me over the years. It is also my desire, in honor of my wife, mother and mother-in-law, to encourage those that need encouragement. It is my hope that the women who read this book will be awakened and empowered to make changes in their lives. Women, you have been asleep for a very long time. The bigger problem is that you do not know that you are asleep. I am hoping that I can appeal to the women that have taken time to study the Bible, that they may reach their own understanding of the Word and avail themselves to a daily women's ministry and God's order. Likewise, I will also need to explain God's order even to the Christian woman for she has lived more by tradition than by God's Word. God so loved the world that He gave this amazing woman to be enjoyed by man. This was an amazing task! Why does man think he needs to change God's order?

Using your amazing design, you, as a woman, will be able to take the rich information contained in this book to highlight things in a very different manner for yourself. You must become the "New You." Don't let past lifestyles hold you back. Women, you have great power in you and awesome blessings ahead of you. Your inner most thoughts have been hampered because of fear. You are fearful that these things will not be fully accepted by men.

Back to my previous statement, "You are this amazing design and you must always keep in mind who you are." All of the problems that you face in life were created by men and they must be solved by men as well. Keep in mind that this book is written by a man. Consider the fact that the man has the answer that can put things in their proper order. This is the way things were initially designed by God. Since both men and women are humans, we make mistakes. However, it is a travesty to continue in this state year after year. It is past time for this amazing woman to make a power move. Remember that sometimes change works in your favor. This change will require that past thinking and past habits no longer be accepted.

Women, you will have to be who God designed you to be! God designed you to be an amazing woman! I have addressed many things in this book that will assist you in reaching your perfect design as God designed you. It is my desire that I will raise your level of understanding. I hope that this knowledge and wisdom is received and appreciated by women everywhere. Women, you are so amazing that it has been very hard for me to understand why it has taken so long for this information to come to fruition. When you factor in all of the media coverage on matters concerning things, relative to cars, wealth, missiles, housing, immigration and other things, you can possibly agree with me on this point. You can understand that the issue between the sexes is covered up by the news media daily.

Some of the problem between the man and the woman is that men have yet to realize their own short comings. Man has not fully understood nor has he put forth an honest effort to understand what God said about the woman. Without this initial understanding you will always miss God's design for you.

I pose a question to the men: "Did God say to treat the woman as though she were the weaker sex?" Men, God did not say that she was the weaker sex. According to the Scriptures, the woman was designed to be the man's help meet. Most men consider women as 50-50 when it comes to financing the household, however, this is not biblical. Allow me to explain this fifty-fifty issue. This fifty-fifty was not a part of God's design because whenever you have a fifty-fifty you have a problem.

Allow me to share one of my personal experiences as an old man with wisdom. I know a couple whose husband is proud to be a fifty-fifty person. This couple argued all the time and about everything. On one occasion, my wife and I were traveling with this particular couple. The airline came out to announce that the flight would not be departing because there was something wrong with the plane. The woman announced that we would all need to stay at a hotel and the plane would leave in the morning. My wife and I went to the hotel with this couple and as the husband began to make the registration he turned to his wife in front of a long line of customers and asked her for her half of the room fee. The wife replied, "I have the money, however, it's not with me right now." Her husband began to argue with her about her share of the hotel fee; in fact, her husband told her to go to the ATM to get her half of the hotel room fee. He did pay for the room, but immediately after paying for the room, he took her to the car and drove us all directly to an ATM where she could withdraw the money. This man was operating in the fifty-fifty mode. A few minutes after this incident we were all tired and hungry and we decided to eat. Well, of course, his wife did not draw out food money so another argument ensued about her half for the food. Then he asked her to write a check out to him for her half of the food. This is just one example of what happens to some couples when they operate in the fifty-fifty mode.

The man, in the beginning, did not have the information that is afforded to men today. Today's man has access to books and magazines that are written about women and their likes and dislikes. This information should help men understand the design of a woman. This information has not created in man a new understanding of who the women really are. The woman has continually suffered at the hands of man because women have always followed their home training or cultural upbringing. However, this type of mentality has continued to keep things going in the same direction for women. The design of a woman has been smothered for centuries. Now is the time for the woman to go for the gold!

The "gold" is just the first accomplishment on the way to their proper place in society. Women have been brain washed from birth to believe that they are less than men. In today's society, you would think that women would begin to look at the spelling of the word that crafted them from the beginning of time. The word "man" describes who he is. The word "wo-man" describes who she is. If the "wo-man" had taken a deep breath she would have noticed that she was an addition to man. With this addition in God's design of a "wo-man," it signifies that she had something added to her. Women, my question to you is, knowing this, How can you be less than man? Man has fooled you all of these years into thinking that a "wo-man" is less than a man. I am honored to have this opportunity to expose man's tactical front. Man's actions are used to show that he has led you wrong from the beginning until this present day. In my eyes, this takes a particular type of courage to face thinking like this and that courage comes from God.

This courage is amazing and women have maintained it to survive this struggle against overwhelming odds. This in itself is truly amazing and the women are to be complemented. Now I must ask this question again, Women are your goals in life worth fighting for? The only answer should be "Yes." Since this is the year of Jubilee, this is exactly the time for all women to begin a new era. Women must fully realize that there will be changes that will take place immediately and some of these immediate changes will be addressed in the ensuing chapters. Being the amazing woman that you are, this will be or should be easily understood by women. When things are continued in the same manner, year after year, the results almost always stay the same. This amazing woman has been living in this depressed state for far too long. Remember, I said that, "Diamonds are made under pressure." You cannot work properly unless you are plugged into the "Power of the Spirit, and have worked hard to know who Jesus is and learn how to treat God's creation." The man who findeth a woman finds a good thing!

When gathering background information to write this book, I began by asking different women questions such as, "How are women studying the written words of the Bible?" I was surprised by some of their responses. A large number of women are not pleased with the treatment that they receive from men at work, their husbands, sons, etc. Yet, these men are proclaiming to be "Legal Christians." I have included the information in this book to let women know the truth about the men they adore. The majority of men in their lives are not "Legal Christians." Only the people who have taken special time in studying the Bible are Legal Christians. This book is written to enlighten both the Christian woman and the "Legal Christian." The "Legal Christian" man will have no problems with the things that are addressed in this book. The women will be able to separate the Christian men from the "Legal Christian" men. The "Legal Christian" man is one who professes to know and has accepted Jesus into his life. You must learn who Jesus really is to become a "Legal Christian." In all of the discussions women have failed to see the difference between "Christian" and "Legal Christian."

I still see two small flaws in the amazing woman. One is that women forget their worth, their actual value in society, and the other is they do not realize their own strengths. Part of this is due to their unique design. The woman was designed to bear children and to forget the pain. Being able to endure something so painful and then forget the pain as soon as she brings forth her new born is truly an amazing strength in the woman, however, this also attributes to her forgetting her true worth when other things around her are just as painful.

Now, I would like to share some information that will open the women's eyes in a very powerful way. Women have shown through academics (such as receiving good jobs, filling leadership positions, being entrepreneurs, and earning more Master's degrees than men), that she is a very intelligent part of creation. What a great accomplishment! We are back at this amazing design and women were designed to fulfill destiny.

The woman has been pulling the plow too long. Now is the time for this amazing design to realize that their time is now! The information that is contained in this book is not meant to be used in the wrong manner. It is my desire that after reading this book the woman will begin to measure her success by what she has gained from the material in this book.

I understand that most of the things that I am writing to women about are rarely discussed and that brings me to another thought: The man needs to give credit where credit is due, and that to the amazing women in his life. For example, men are usually seeking better employment or a better position than their present job. It's usually the woman who is driving them to seek a higher position and it's usually the woman that fills out the applications for employment and even develops and types resumes for their men to get better jobs. This is something that is usually understated by the man that his help meet helped him to move in to the position he now occupies. I also believe that women are usually more adept at doing creative writing than men are. This is another gift of women that is rarely realized or stated by men. That's why I stated earlier, "Credit should always be given where credit is due." Men are always boasting about their accomplishments, but they rarely state the fact that their wives helped them to achieve them. I understand that this can be very frustrating to the woman. Man wants to dominate the woman rather than be the leader of his household.

CHAPTER THREE

The Uncertain Period

Since we now have an understanding of the beginning and the design of women, we must understand that a period of uncertainty followed these beginnings. The wisdom and knowledge that is contained in the Scriptures is the best way to understand who the woman is. First you look at the Scriptures and you find these words: "He who findeth a wife findeth a good thing" (Proverbs 18:22). For this phrase to be in the Scriptures, it is an indication that God looks at the woman as being very, very special.

Now, let's go back and search the Scriptures and see where you can find the same saying in reference mmmmm   j
jj to the man. This phrase signifies that the woman should be accepted the way God sees her. God also stated in His Word that, "Men should love their wives as He loves the church." These sayings are given to

us for an example of just how special God has designed women. She should be the most desired and precious gift a man can have in his life. This desire should be greater than precious stones or gold. This in itself should make the woman realize who she really is. Women should stop letting men dominate them, and they should not let men treat them as though they are not precious. Women have been treated poorly for such a long time that they have started to believe that this is the way God designed them.

Women are taught from a very early age that men are the leaders or head of the household. This is the way God intended it to be, however, men have not followed the precepts of God and have not adhered to God's order of things and the design of life in which God intended for it to be on this planet. The woman is designed to be a help meet to the man. She was not designed to be dominated by man. The men of this world have gotten the design wrong. Men think that women are not to be treated as equal with different duties. The Bible states that, "Women should be obedient." If you read the Bible it also states that the man should be obedient as well. His obedience is directed to God who is his head. Man answers to God. Men read the Bible and immediately think that God's Word is only meant for one of the sexes and not for both. When God used the above phrase He was talking about men and women.

The most difficult task in life is to get man to understand how he should treat the woman. Man has failed to realize how much better his situation in life would be if he would utilize the wisdom and knowledge that is in God's word about the design of a woman. To the women I say, you should begin to gravitate back to your original design. Women were designed to be mothers, wives, daughters, teachers, business leaders, singers, dancers and almost anything you can possibly think of. Women who have taken on different roles in society have been very successful. I think that the woman should be proud of her accomplishments; some of which were achieved without the support of the man and without man being pleased with her accomplishments. The woman, even though dominated by man, has managed to find her way in society. Now that she is coming into the knowledge of who she is and what she can achieve, this should make her finally realize the sacrifices that it took for her to be in the position that she now enjoys.

Women have yet to reach their full potential in life.

So I say to the woman, As you read this book and as it assists you in realizing exactly who you are, I pray you will find renewed strength to stop going in the direction you are going. I hope this book will empower you to change directions and improve your life. This is the time for you to step back and look at your design. While you are looking at your design you should start today in making changes in your lifestyle. Go back to the things that are important to you. Strive to do the things that make you feel good on the inside. It could be something as simple as time alone, getting your nails done, going to the beauty salon, buying a new dress, or finishing your college degree. Begin now to work on the things that make you happy and feel special. I'd like to share this example with you, and you can see from this example that this works both ways. My wife walks into the house from working all day and she notices that I was still in my home clothes, my "knock-around-the-house-clothes." She says, "Why didn't you dress in a nice shirt and pants? Why do you have on those old shoes, when you have all those new shoes?" My reply to her was, "Why do I need to change clothes when I'm not going anywhere?" To which she replied, "It's for me!" So I went and changed my clothing to please my wife because if this pleases her then we have peace within the home and it also pleases me to please her.

I am sure that there are many women who are now living with fellows who appear to be men that need to be rescued by them. I am writing this book to inform the women that perhaps they have never been taught by their fathers exactly how men are supposed to treat women. For most of the man's life he has been doing the same thing—treating women as though they were less than he. Most men whom I have come in contact with seem to have this same type of thinking about women. Since men have not understood the difference between women and themselves from the beginning of time, it is finally time for someone to fully explain in plain language what God did from the spiritual realm.

God gave some things to the wo-man which he did not give to the man, neither does the man have the right to treat his teammate differently because she is playing first base and he is the pitcher. They both have positions on the same team. I am surprised that men did not nor do not understand why the life span of one that was made from him lives longer than he does, especially since he is suppose to be the stronger one. This indicates that man has gotten the message that God has written in His Word totally wrong. Bless his heart. God said in His Word that, "When a man findeth a wife he findeth a good thing." I also understand that man's initial thoughts reference to God's Word, but he must move on further in the Scriptures where it states that, "You must study the Scriptures to show thyself approved unto God" (II Timothy 2:15). If a man does this he will not be lacking in understanding, knowledge and wisdom to rightly divide the Word of Truth.

When a man is not treated as the king of his home it's because he does not fully understand what is required of him to be "King of his castle." When you fail to treat your mate with respect and most of all as an equal who has been designed to help you with your shortcomings, then most men will find themselves following their wives instead of being "King." For instance, let me share this scenario with you regarding my parents.

My mother would say to my Dad, "He's not going to be lying to you." She was referring to me when she made that statement. When my Father would hear her talking this way the veins in his forehead looked as though they would pop and he would become angry. Even though he was a forceful and proud man, my Mother used to take the lead in the family. She was adamant that I would not be like my father. She then demanded of him to find a better job which he did. In fact, in this scenario you can see that my mother was the "Queen of the castle."

So women can be the force in the household when they demand it! My mother demanded her equality in raising the children, in going to church and in making the decisions in our home no matter the consequences and there were many. This type of situation calls for respect and help and is a two way action. You trust me, I trust you. You should get in the habit of realizing that your wife is your greatest asset. You (man), need her and she needs you. Men should be grateful that they have someone to help them. Here again let me share a true story with you.

Red and Annie are married and have been married for several years. Annie loves Red and what Red does not understand is just how much Annie loves him. Red walked out of the door of his home, got into his car, and began to back out of the driveway when he heard his phone ringing. Red became angry when he realized that it was Annie calling him, especially since he had just left the house. He thought to himself that Annie was constantly bothering him. What Red didn't realize was that Annie was constantly thinking of him and this should have made him feel good?

This kind of closeness just upsets most men. Men often get upset by the things their wives do for them which they may think is totally ridiculous, whereas his wife feels she is performing a labor of love. Man feels this way because he is not wired the same way as his wife. Instead of accepting the closeness, most men like Red, reject this type of closeness. They consider their woman nagging them, not trusting them, or trying to control them when the woman just wanted to know where he would be and when she could expect him. It has nothing to do with jealousy, control or anger, but a need to know where he is. Is that not her right, men?

Most things that have been said and written about women have usually been written from a male perspective. According to the structure that is mandated in the Bible man is suppose to be keeping things "in order" until Jesus comes back. Man has not fully understood his role. Jesus did not leave man as the leader, so he would lead the woman astray. From the beginning, man has participated in things that continually degrade the woman, while the woman has participated in the life-giving process of all mankind. Having done this, you would think that man would praise her and try to understand the uniqueness in the design of her character instead of always trying to say or do things that cheapen her or make her seem inferior to him. Men make subtle statements about women most of the time. They say and make comments like, "Is that a woman driving. Then I'd better get out of the way!" This scenario has continued throughout the ages.

Men down through the ages have grossly misunderstood what God made for them. Men for the most part do not realize nor understand that they are in error in their treatment of women. It has been my observation that today's woman, based on terrible treatment for years and years, finds it very, very difficult to adjust to a man who is truly good and understanding. However, sometimes the shoe is on the other foot. She takes his goodness and kindness for weakness and exploits it. Also, based on the tradition of women always seeing men and husbands out with other women, she has now began to take on the vices of men as she exits the house as well. Based on Bible principles, a woman should think of herself more highly. I am not saying that all women have copied the ways of man. I am saying that, presently the system is terrible. Women, based on the world's system, will do almost anything. They do not know how beautifully they have been designed. God took time out of His schedule to design a woman specifically for the man and until this day man has not fully realized what God has done for him. God does not make mistakes. If you, as a man, have not realized that the woman was not a mistake, then you should begin to get it together when it comes to the treatment of women.

Men, let me share this with you. When I took a look at myself, I discovered that I had no respect for women and I certainly did not see her as an equal, neither did I respect my wife's opinion. For example, I did not want my wife to wear wigs. One day I found my wife wearing a wig. I immediately pulled the wig off her head and began to stomp on it. I mean, I began to jump on it like it was a wild animal. I didn't care whether or not she liked wearing wigs; I was the man and I did not want my wife to wear a wig and I was having it my way. Then I began to study the Bible, and it was not until I began to study the Bible that I began to change my perspective of women. I found a better way to treat women and you can too.

The differences between a man and a woman can never be changed. However, men can begin to view the woman as an equal and a help meet in life. Men and women are always discussing things that are not really wrong or right—the differences only lie in how each sex interprets things. The difference between men and women will keep them from dealing with something that you only think is a problem, when really there is no existing problem at all—just the opinion of the sexes. You, as a person, should keep this information in mind at all times and remember it as you enter into future conversations with the opposite sex. Two people will never exactly be alike. You must always respect each other's differences at all times especially when the difference comes into play during discussions and mutual conversations. At this point, I say to the man and woman, it's time to clear the slate and start fresh. Share your gifts and talents instead of bickering with one another. Start listening to each other with an open mind and heart. This will enable each of you to start looking at the God in each of you. Always dwell on the good things about your mate. Neither of you are without fault.

To the man I say, stop throwing stones at her and start thinking about the way God thinks of her. If you practice the things written in this book, no matter where you may roam, you will find the sun and rain, but you will never feel alone because you will be in the company of each other. The good thoughts about each other will keep you from feeling the absences when you are away from your mate for any period of time. Thinking good thoughts gives you the feeling of closeness. When this is done on a regular and consistent basis your greetings at home will be so great that you will find that you will unknowingly be hurrying home to be greeted so graciously by your wife. This will move your relationship into a more meaningful and close relationship towards each other. You will begin to think about how blessed you are to have each other in your lives.

Now let's discuss a phrase I believe men should do away with and that phrase is, "hen pecked." This is a phrase used by men who are unhappy in their relationship with their wives or close companion. When a man is very considerate of his wife's and children's way of presenting things to him he is labeled hen pecked. When he remains calm and handles the matter with kindness and respect, and he shows great love and respect for those he cares about, he is really hen pecked. When a man is very respectful with his wife and the way he treats his mother, then he is called hen pecked. When a man repeatedly says, "Yes, dear," in the presence of his buddies they take the respectful gesture as being "hen pecked." Is it then we feel we need to be a man by being rude? No, it is not easy being a "Yes, dear," man, but who do you live with? Do you want to be right or happy?

Men, you should never listen to people that do not understand the design of a woman. Women were designed to be different from men. She has some of the same things that were in the design of a man. Since both of them have differences, they should both be very respectful to each other. I ask you to, stop blowing the differences between the two sexes out of proportion. Begin now to make statements to each other such as, "Can we discuss this?" Or "Can we work this out?" Say things like, "I understand that we are both different yet we should be considerate of each other's feelings and opinions." I will say that neither of you should begin to think that because you thought of it first, that your mate should say, okay, right away.

Learn to respect each other's opinions. Men, let us learn to listen to women before we try to fix the situation or dismiss her ideas as stupid or too emotional. What I have learned over the years is that learning to accept each other's faults and choosing to celebrate each other's differences is one of the most important keys to creating a healthy, growing and lasting relationship. Let me give you an example of a help meet.

If a woman keeps and cleans the house during a five day week, then she has completed her week's work. If this is true, then why is Saturday or Sunday his day off? When does the helper get to be off? This indicates that since they both are off on the weekends then the work should be shared. Since they are both in this relationship together then why are these duties left mostly for the woman to take care of? There is no place in the Bible that states that there is a higher work demand for women than men. Somehow, the man has gotten the family structure completely wrong.

In this book, I'd like for women to take a look at the past, present, and the future. If the woman would take a closer look at the world as a whole, she would begin to be able to better understand the situation that presently exists. For starters, the men are the appointed "leaders." The women should get their dictionaries and carefully define what a "leader" is. I will start at the top. President Barack Obama has been selected by the people of the United States to be a leader of the free world. This means that he is to adopt policies and make decisions that are good for the people that he has been appointed to lead. This appointment was made and designed by the people of the free world. This type of design has been repeated for years and years. The various departments are in position to keep this government focused on its leadership.

I hope that the women who read this book will begin to understand that during times of change going on in the country, women should try to improve their image as well, especially in the workplace. During the years of men going off to fight the wars, women were given more of an opportunity to learn many jobs that were mainly designed with men in mind. This gave the women the chance and also the opportunity to show to the world that they could do the same type of work that the men could do. Some of the jobs that the women were doing were things that women liked. A vast majority of these women liked the jobs. The pay was one of the things that the women liked most. The biggest disappointment was that the employers of those women were paying the women less than the amount that men were paid. Since the woman was doing things such as providing for the family and taking care of the house and the car, she began to consider moving into other places in the work force.

This period in life gave the women a chance to prove that she could take care of the family and do other things as well. This lets the world know and see what things were in the woman that had not been tapped into. The woman knew that she could do all of these things. These inner abilities were being suppressed by the "macho man." The man has tried to do things in a way that would appeal to the world that this is a man's world. This is one of the most outrageous statements ever stated by man.

I cannot fathom how the religious leaders in this world could allow this thinking to be lived and taught in religious settings. The men are the biggest leaders in the religious world. This is not in error based on how God designed the order of things. God designed the man to be a leader. When a leader is leading in the order that was designed by God he must lead according to Biblical Scriptures.

I will be amazed if a true Bible scholar were to show me in the Scriptures that God designed his mother as a lesser individual than he himself was. Man will have a real problem trying to explain his actions on earth toward the woman. The woman found out that she was capable of doing just about anything. The women moved into areas where they were not fully accepted. This empowered them to keep pressing on. She had a threefold problem that she had not fully realized or thought about. She had not considered the fact that her father was a man. When she started to undertake these new tasks in life, the father, husband and her employer early in life would all be men. These individuals have been a hindrance to woman.

Take a good look at what I'm saying to you in this book. I'm saying that, you are better than that! You have had your talents suppressed for years and years. This in itself is what I consider proof positive. When you have moved into this position, you have arrived. This reminds me of the title of the movie, "Are We There Yet?" The answer to that related to the woman is, "Yes." We are there. I want to further emphasize that the Bible was written for the believers. All of the people in the world are not believers. According to Scripture, all people are God's creation, but all people are not God's children.

Therefore, the woman who is not a believer will have a difficult time fully understanding what is being written about the woman in this book. Women who for their whole lifetime were taught the Bible and also instructed by the leader will also have to take a closer look at the Bible. It will be very easy for the women that have studied the Bible and acquired wisdom, knowledge and understanding to understand this book. Be sure to read this Scripture, "In all of your getting get understanding," so that you can rightly divide the Word of Truth. The way to divide the Word of Truth is by every Word that proceeds out of the mouth of Jesus.

I want every woman in the whole world to consider my statement relative to Jesus. I want all women to notice that it did not say every word that proceeds out of the mouth of man. I did not say every word that proceeds out of the mouth of woman. I am hoping that by writing this book and making it easier to understand that the woman will finally realize and consider being the woman as designed by the Creator, God the Almighty.

During the last sixty years the woman has made remarkable strides against all odds. You, the woman, will be admitted into the hall of fame on earth if you begin to organize. You must get back to the order that you were designed for. This will be the greatest accomplishment in the history or life of the woman. This will be a difficult change for the women that are making large sums of money. Men have shown that they are very pleased with many of the things that the women are doing, however, they are threatened by them and fear losing control.

I am addressing things relating to God's order. I am trying to open the spiritual eyes of these remarkable women. One of the main causes of blindness in the spiritual eyes of the women is because they have been following what men have told them. The man feels that he was designed to be the "Leader" in this world. The Devil has been leading him in the domination direction. This has been bad for the woman because she has had to endure all of the unnecessary things used by man to suppress her inner abilities. She has had her careers hampered or failed to take a higher paying job with travel which took her from the home. This is one of the major changes that has taken place in the last thirty years. During these uncertain years, the woman has pushed forward. I would think that the woman in the latest era of this new technology has enabled her to move into many new types of jobs in society. The woman has been praying for the family and the man on the road to a much better life. The woman was designed to have strong family ties. There is nothing greater than a mother's love. During these uncertain periods in life, there have been far more men walking away from the family. The main responsibility for the man was him being designed by God to be the leader.

I would think that the woman would have taken a closer look at what is written in the Book of Life. Instead of doing this, the woman has continued in pretty much the same state—living as a lesser individual. Women have become content to be the lesser individual, yet her thoughts are burdened with people perceiving her as someone who is not taking care of her family, not cooking or cleaning, not working a 9 to 5 job, not being home for homework, etc. Yet she must work outside the home to help with household finances. Man wants to be the leader; but he wants help with household chores, finances and medical expenses. Women are shunned if they fail to be the perfect idea of a mother, set by society and man. Can woman be an equal partner or is she still being asked to be the major bread winner, the super Mom, the super maid, the super sex partner, the beautiful wife with all her hair in place and body fit? Yet, after all this she is not supposed to be equal. Ladies, is this God's design for you? You are blessed. You are His. Where should your value be?

CHAPTER FOUR

Modesty

Considering the mood in the world towards women, you would think that modesty would come very easily. Instead, the woman has taken a very different role. The information I present throughout this writing is not referenced to all women. There are many, many women who are front runners when it comes to modesty. You must always keep in mind that the first impression means a great deal. You, the woman, are dealing with a society that has rated you unfairly. Now is the time for you to show society that you can recapture the place you held in society for so long. This in itself proves that you have the necessary inner abilities to return to the modest woman.

The most admired women are the modest women. Today's woman has allowed herself to be viewed by most men as sex symbols. Since we are living in a civilized society one would think that all women would consider the natural laws and also spiritual laws. The Father looks at the woman as the style setter for the family. I am sure that the woman has noticed that women are truly style conscious individuals. Knowing that women are the style setters, would equate to the woman understanding that she will be held accountable for leading the world into fashions and trends that are totally unacceptable.

The woman has moved from being modest to the role of trying to see how sexy she can dress. This is not the way God wanted women to be portrayed. Women seem to think of themselves as sex symbols. This kind of thinking is absolutely ridiculous. This type of thinking has done more to harm her image. Your image is really part of who you are. Now that you are planning your power move, some of your styles will have to be modified. I see many styles that make it very difficult for the woman to be able to bend down or to sit in front or across from other people when they are in places like the airport or in hotel lobbies. I think that women should begin to realize that men are attracted more to things that they cannot see. Remember that the countries where women are completely covered, have larger families than some of the families in countries where women dress almost uncovered. Men will be attracted to women regardless of the dress style.

Now that women are finding out who they really are, the move towards more modest dress will be necessary in the coming years. I can see this modern day woman taking on the challenge of becoming the woman that takes charge of her new beginning. When you move into the places that are mostly held by men, the required dress and style will be changed. Some jobs require that you wear uniforms while others require that you wear business attire. I see women in their military uniforms and I think that they are very sexy and gracious. There is something very special to me about a woman in uniform. The women that are in special attire in hospitals are considered very, very special as well. The women that are in special attire on many of the airlines are very, very sexy as well as women who dress modestly in other countries. Contrary to popular belief, "real men," are more attracted to modestly dressed women. When women are scantily dressed they will attract more attention. This does not equate to the meaning of attraction. When women realize that men are more attracted to the modestly dressed woman they will connect with this information and will lead much happier future lives. The woman must start to realize how great it is to be a "real woman"—the woman she was born to be!

Let's take a look at the Queen of England. She is one of the most respected women in the world. She is also the most photographed woman in the world and her dress is always modest. Also of note are the women who have their own TV shows—they are very modestly dressed as entertainers and talk show hosts and they are very successful. These women are admired by all men. For instance, most of us can recall Margaret Thatcher, the former Prime Minister of Great Britain. She did not dress like most of the modern day women; in fact, she dressed very modestly and professionally. However, the modern day women in America are against women wearing long dresses, yet at special functions they wear long gowns. They believe in modesty, but only on special occasions.

The most highly respected women in the world are the modestly dressed women. The military women who are dressed modestly at all times show that men have the same desire for modestly dressed women as well. Let's take a look at the problems they have in the military with the men in the military who are constantly after them. This lets you know that modestly dressed women are still very attractive.

To the women I must say this, women, you were designed to protect your self image. Mothers were to be modest in all things. When you are raising children the children are looking at the mother very, very closely. In today's world the mothers are mostly not very modest. Most of this is due to the many, many years of being exploited by man. Just because women are on the TV, the Internet, Youtube etc., scantily dressed doesn't mean this is a normal way to present oneself. I don't think that the woman has taken the time to realize that a modest woman is the most desired woman on the planet earth!

The woman has been given a choice in life relative to a special relationship with man. She has almost always taken the road of trying to please the man. This has been a very, very difficult task for the woman. With her devotion to her husband and family she is still considered as not being equal to the man. This has caused many, many heartaches because she cannot understand how he is able to treat her as though she is not special in his life. This leads to permanent tension between couples. The women that I have discussed this with are in the thousands. I have been researching this mistreatment of women by men with men also. When you ask the men and you must put the question in a way in which he does not know he is being asked this question. For example, bring up the topic of being equal to the woman and most of the men that I have talked with will say, 'no, they are not equal.' I have found only approximately 1 out of 100 men that consider their significant other as being equal to them. So, most men see women as lesser people.

When the woman begins to take a good look at the things that are said, she will begin to realize who she really is. Women are very, very special, and therefore you should always act the part, as a blessed, valued, virtuous and equal woman.

Modesty is the best way to go. God intended for women to be modest. This generation has gotten completely out of the place that God intended for it to be in. Man has led woman so far from the woman's intended purpose which she was designed to be when he began to think that she was designed as a sex symbol. Her sexuality was designed for her husband and her pleasure not for the front pages of books, TV, magazines, etc. You, as women, have given into the leader who has always defined you as being less than him. Women have bought into this type of behavior for years and years, now you have decided that his way is right. His way has enabled women to earn lots of money quickly. With your earning power you still are not consider as an equal with the man. Even your elected officials vote as though you are the weaker sex. How many years did it take for the woman to get the right to vote?

God will empower the woman as soon as she returns to her original design, because empowerment comes along with modesty. So, women, stop using your body as a primary form of communication. It is time to become that virtuous woman that God made you to be. This woman was spoken about in the book of Proverbs. You should love and embrace every blessing that God has blessed you with spiritually, physically and emotionally. You need to start speaking with more conviction. I have looked at various shows on TV and read books and stories written by women, and in reading these things, it has drawn my attention to these findings. When women are on the TV shows and interviews they are adding to the way that men view women. If you listen very closely to the women that are always discussing situations that happen between many married couples, you will find that the women are making statements about the marriage relationship based on the way men think about women. They, for the most part, are talking as though they are not quite an equal to man. This adds fuel to the fire and is just one of the many reasons that this unequal situation has continued to flourish. It is time for the woman to realize who she really is and begin to live the way God planned it. Women should begin to look at themselves as very special individuals who should demand that men give them the respect that God designed them to have.

When the women begin to think like this and demand godly respect, this moves the women to a modest way of dressing as well because they will begin to think of themselves as God designed them to be. Women, I must say to you, stop wearing clothes that show everything! If women continue to dress in dresses that are not modest, the situation will continue to be as it is presently. Remember, you are now presently considered an unequal because every billboard has the woman represented scantily dressed. Dressing properly is one of the things that should be considered by the woman. Women you are considered as precious by your Maker. Now that you are reading this book you should find something that hits home and that is one of my desires for writing this book. If I were considered to be a precious gem, then I would try to present myself in that likeness. The woman has been exploited for so long that she has forgotten her real design and worth.

Take a look at how God designed you . You are the most precious design in all the universe and you should take time to consider how God created you and gifted you and put in His special qualities that make you a woman. Once you take these factors into consideration you should began to modify your life according to the standards in which you were created.

There is another subject that I'd like to present to the women as well and I'm quite serious regarding this topic. Women, when it comes to attending church you are completely over looking your design when it comes to the rules of dressing. This indicates that it is time for the women in the sanctuary to pull these women aside and to remind them that modesty is everything. Unfortunately, we are living in a time when everyone is afraid to say, this dress is unacceptable. This problem or situation should be addressed by someone in or outside of the church in a godly manner. Yes, God said, "Come as you are," but the attire is important. Ladies, just cover up. I am not the fashion police but I know how a man thinks. God is a God of order, so heed His Word.

Some of the information in this book is written for

the supposedly Biblical scholars. I am very, very surprised by the scholars that operate in high places. These places are the megachurches. The top Baptist ministers, the Catholic Church and various other ministries. These ministers are leaders in the world. Also there are other leaders in the political world. Let's start with the president. The world has had to deal with the governors, the congressmen, the House and the Senate leaders. With all of these different leaders and organizations you would think that we would not have this unequal treatment towards women. The problems that men have with women exist because they are going on in high places. It has been going on for so long that the followers of these leaders include many women. I must note that most of the women in high places dress very modestly. I think this is due partly because the women in high places are independent thinkers. When you become a leader with certain assigned duties you remove yourself from the dress that would seem to be degrading to women if worn.

Let's take a look at most of the women in high places that are married to men. We will start with the Queen of England, Secretary of State, Margaret Thatcher, and the megachurch First Ladies. These women evidently feel or understand that the men will have more respect for a modestly dressed woman. This dress wear is a very big form of exploitation. In your quest to be accepted into the places that were initially designed for men by men, you failed to keep your design in the proper order. Women, your present day styles are not in the proper order. You are clearly being led into thinking that you are only a sex symbol. I would like to address this to all of the most prominent women in society today. The women in your present day society are usually modestly dressed. Let's look at some of them. Take for instance, the Queen of England, Oprah Winfrey, Hillary Clinton, and Michelle Obama, these women are considered to be "First Ladies." Also there are "first ladies" married to megachurch ministers and they all dress in a very modest way. This should equate to why modesty is still for women in today's society.

Why have women allowed the man to think that they are not capable of being in control of their own dress style? Women, there remains the old saying, "Dress to impress." Or, "If you got it, flaunt it." Well women, what is this getting you? No, I am not telling you to wear turtleneck sweaters and baggy jeans. Women, I am saying dress to impress and honor God and all else will fall into place. Define the word beautiful in your mind as God designed you. Women, is your dress representing His design?

The design God set for you is blessed, virtuous and beloved. Check yourself in God's Word. Are you dressing yourself or is the world dressing you? You would not allow your mother to dress you, then why let the world?

CHAPTER FIVE

Marriage

H e who findeth a woman findeth a good
thing." This statement comes directly from
the Bible, and it is one statement seems
mind boggling to many men. I cannot understand
how all of these supposedly Christian men who are
considered Legal Christians, do not understand God's
Word. Yet, they claim to be a leader and also a scholar
of the principles of the Word of God. I challenge
men to study the design of the woman. Evidently,
men have not studied God's design of a woman. As
you are reading the words and definitions in this
book, please pay close attention to the things that
are being addressed in The Design of a Woman.
The things that are being addressed are the things
that have been put at the bottom of the list of things
that need to be addressed.

Women, take your time as you read this chapter. This
chapter includes things that are rarely discussed

among men. The only men who will acknowledge this about his woman or about women at large are men who I call "Legal Christians." A Legal Christian is a man that fully understands what Solomon was saying when He said, "He who findeth a wife findeth a good thing."

Man needs to understand what a powerful and special undertaking God did when He designed a "help meet," for him (Genesis 2:18). The woman must first go to the book of Genesis when Adam and Eve were in the Garden of Eden. They were assigned specific things to do and things not to do. This Book compares the beginning of time when women were created to this present day.

There are very few men who really understand that Eve was not put in charge. Adam was the one who was to keep the order. Go back and check the Scriptures out for yourself (Genesis 1:26). Man is very slow when it comes to fully understanding who Jesus is. Men read about Him, they talk about Him, they attend church, but they are usually in that "Doubting Thomas" mode when it comes to Jesus. Also, man becomes a "Doubting Thomas" when it comes to understanding the way God designed the woman. Women are usually found doing most things that would please the man. Genesis 3:16 says that a woman's desire "shall be to thy husband." Men are not usually doing things to please the woman. He is usually doing things that would please himself or take care of his needs. This is where man and woman are very, very different.

The nature of a woman is to please man. This is her natural ability given to her by God. This nature of a woman has been abused by men from the beginning of time. Look at Adam—he blamed Eve for his sin. It is always the woman's fault. Men have focused on the fact that he is the "man." Men for the most part think of themselves as being superior, therefore, he can do things he considers a "man's thing." This is not always pleasing to the woman. She feels that she should have been included in his decision or at least listened to before he made that decision. This is considered normal behavior for men in general.

Most men hang on to the Scripture in the Bible that states that the woman should "honor and obey" her husband. The man has failed to realize that the woman has both sexes within her. For the woman to endure this type of treatment for so long shows that the woman has developed resilience that is really mind boggling. After having endured all of this, the woman still has to remind her husband that he is not dealing with a child but with a wife and a lifetime partner.

Men, you must respect her and consider her opinions, her wants, her desires, her career choices, and many other decisions in her life. Women know things will be different by a large margin. The reason is she is not a man. You must always keep in mind that your wife is a woman with very different views, emotions and opinions. This is really not a bad thing as men seem to think. When you have two minds working on the same thing you always come up with a better solution. Two minds are always better than one.

I have not included all of the biblical Scriptures in this book, although men need to find these Scriptures so that they may better understand the Bible. The Bible contains the reason you, as a husband, should never say to your wife, 'you are less than me. I give the orders.' She is your help meet, not your child. This kind of reasoning leads to unnecessary arguments that are totally not needed in a marriage. When you are out shopping together, you, as the man and head of the family, must keep in mind that your wife is not a man and that her design is far different from yours. When you and your wife are selecting items for purchase, you should always keep in mind that she is different. Respect the differences, consider and expect the differences, and always come to an agreement that both of you can live with. Man needs to understand that there are a lot of differences between men and women. Armed with this information about God's design of a woman, the man should begin to condition himself to listen, and yes, to honor the differences that are unique between the woman and man.

Men, when you are engaged and then you take the "Oath of Marriage," there are many things you must change immediately. You have become joined with a wife. You must acknowledge the change. Now, there are two people making decisions about the family. Your wife was designed to be by your side at all times. This is one of the things usually overlooked by men. Many men get married and they want to live as though they are still single. This is very, very frustrating for the wife and children involved. Instead of frustrating your wife, men, you should be trying to please her. Men, you should be pleased to have a help meet who is willing to work with you in spite of your ways; she is generally trying to make a good relationship between the two of you.

Women have extended talents as a help meet. She is your helper and should be treated as a help meet. Men usually do not understand the phrase help meet. Men, your wife is your marriage partner who was designed as a help meet. Women have the burden of meeting certain obligations such as rearing a family; she is the woman in the family and her husband is the man in the family.

Men, women are supposed to be your help meet. You must understand that your wife has many roles, first as a wife, then as a bread winner, provider of child care for your children, and she also takes care of things when you are incapacitated or not capable of doing them. She is supposed to be by your side at all times. She is not your child, therefore you should treat her accordingly. Treat her as a helper, someone of value with rights as a partner with equal privileges. You should always give consideration to her input into family matters. The two leaders of the family should consider each other's opinions. The Bible states, "You should treat her as though she is the weaker sex" (I Peter 3:7). God did not say that she is weaker than man. The Bible has mandated how you must treat her. All things that are written in the Bible are commands from God and should be given heed to because He makes the final decisions about

His creation. He created her with you in mind.

This is what I am trying to do: I'm trying to sow the truth into the lives, hearts, and minds of man. The woman was designed to keep order in the family and to aid in maintaining the health of the family. She loves her home; she wants to decorate the house; she wants to decorate the office; she wants to cook, which expresses the importance of family life. She gives life by birthing children; she helps the man with all of the things he is obligated to do. Man has been labeled the leader in every situation. Over the years, he has decided that the woman should be doing things in the family that were first assigned to him. He consistently forgets the phrase, "Treat her as though she were the weaker sex." God put that phrase in the Bible for man to better understand how God views the woman. He views her as being very, very special. She was designed to be special. She was not designed to be dominated or exploited due to the nature of her kindness or the subservient ways she was given at birth. Since women are most often viewed as caring, loving, nurturing, giving unselfishly, emotional, and most often will give in first in an argument, these attributes have been taken as weakness by the man.

Men constantly take advantage of this design. This type of action is not pleasing to God because He designed her to do these things for man and his family. Most certainly, men will be judged by their treatment of women. Man must remember that God did not give him the things that he gave the woman. She was given the ability to have both male and female traits. Man should take a moment to think about this. She will work within the home, outside the home, suffer discrimination in the workplace and dust herself off in many instances and keep on going strong. All men should wonder why and take note of this awesome nurturing ability of women. Nurturing and taking care of you, the children, her parents and those who need her are of the utmost importance in her life. Men hardly ever think about the way their mother nurtured them when they were growing up. Men, you must always realize that this is one of the woman's many talents given to them at birth.

You must always observe and cherish her many talents. She usually thinks faster and without judgment more than men. This talent is sometimes frustrating to men. Most men fail to realize that she was designed to be a wife, mother, nurturer, and equipped with the ability to accept the blame, bear the children in pain, and still be at her best at all times. All women were designed to be mothers. With that understanding, she should be treated with the same respect that you would extend to your mother. When a wife is treated like a mother she will respond in ways towards her husband that will just be unbelievable. That is a lady or what I call a virtuous blessed woman, who needs to feel loved, respected, praised, and honored above all the roles God designed her to be. There is no life without her. God ordained that she would be honored and taken care of. When Jesus was dying on the cross, He asked John to take care of His mother (John 19:26, 27). When God needed water, He asked a woman to bring Him some (John 4:7). It was a woman who washed His feet with her hair (John 11:2). So what makes man think the woman is not to be honored?

Women must always demand respect from men. Men should always treat a lady with respect. When men constantly treat women like ladies they are and will begin to respond affectionately and with respect toward those men. Men complain about women not acting like ladies. Now look around and observe: men are the ones who are not acting like mature men in the presence of women. Men, as a whole, are not aware of how they really look in the eyes of a lady.

Men very rarely think about how they look or act through the eyes of a lady. Based on the design of the woman and the man, we see the woman as a giver. Basically, she is always loving and doing things to please the man. The woman has many duties including buying things in support of the family; she voluntarily assists in whatever needs to be done to keep her family moving forward. She also pays essential household bills.

Keeping all of this in mind, the man, as a general rule, does not consider her as being an individual who was created equal to him. She is equal with different assignments given to her from within by Almighty God who designed her. God had this in His perfect plan when He created man and woman. However, man has exploited the plan which God intended for the sexes and now the time has come for man to take a step back and look at what he has been doing to and for the woman.

The woman has taken on a completely different role because she has a very hard time following the leadership of man who is out of his position as God so designed. Man thinks that it is all about him being the leader. Man believes he is the one who has the power to treat women as he pleases. He does not understand the phrase, "The meek shall inherit the earth." This means that meekness is to be accepted by all.

The relationship and bonding is an innate ability that is a major part of a woman's make up. She has been exploited from the beginning of time. Men are accustomed to treating women in a certain manner based on the past. This treatment, or what man's male descendants did, is not in accordance with and not based on the design of God. God designed the woman with certain special talents that are most often seen as her being kind and caring. These observations are correct, but God did not give these talents to the woman for man to use against her as if she is weaker than he. He gave her these special talents to be treated as though she were the weaker sex.

The Bible states, that 'you should treat all women as though they were the weaker sex.' Any time you find things like this stated in the Bible, it means that God has commanded man to understand what He commanded of him. When you begin to understand God's relationship with the woman, then you will begin to understand that mothers have always been very, very loyal to their children. This is a great quality in a woman. When we take a look at the men whom the women have reared through the years, the men have become leaders in companies, the government, and other various organizations within society. They seem to take on a different view or perspective of the woman who reared them. I sometimes wonder if the politicians in the United States of America with all of its capabilities do not realize that many things are possible because of a woman.

There was long ago an issue dealing with women's equality as it related to the woman's right to vote. How long did it take before man allowed women to vote? Now take a look at the Military. How long did it take men to decide to let women enter the Military? Women are in various jobs or positions in this society, yet they are not considered equal. Even during divorce there is a very, very big argument when the word equal comes up—equal distribution or the dividing up of things accumulated during the marriage. This shows that the man did not agree with the vow that he made when they were getting married.

The Minister always addresses the fact that they have now become "one." How do you agree to become "One," with another whom you do not consider to be equal to yourself? I want all of the "real men," that will read these statements that are written in this book to examine themselves. You may be amazed to find that you are not the leader that God planned for in this earth. To make an error with man could be considered a mistake. I would like to know, how you (a man of God) can think that God has accepted the error in your ways? If you check out the Scriptures you will find that God assigned Adam, the man, to be a leader. When God assigns you to a position it is commanded that you do it. The Scriptures also state that, "You, man, do not change His orders, not one tilt."

According to what is written in the Bible (Rev. 22:18-19), men will have to be forgiven of many things and especially his unkind treatment towards the woman. Ladies, remind your man of the duties of a man instead of degrading him. Let him know that you expect your man to be the family leader. Also, let him know that he should be a leader in the community and in business matters as well. Always remember that men are as sensitive as women, they just hide their sensitivity very, very well. I am a very sensitive man, but you would never have known this other than for my writing it in this book.

Men pride themselves on being macho, cool and in control. The man and the woman both have human feelings. Usually the woman is more likely to show or display her feelings or emotions during most situations. Men are full of the macho actions rather than allowing their true feelings to show. Ladies, please be careful when you are looking at unrealistic TV programs, listening to single females, unsaved or bitter women who are out to destroy your image as a good woman. The news and other things that are viewed on TV have a direct impact on new marriages that are not doing very well. Newly married couples spend a lot of time looking at movies and TV programs. Understand that the way women are portrayed in movies and on TV programs is not the way women are suppose to be as the help meet in the family. Women are to be supporters in the family makeup.

Most of today's men look to the woman as a 50/50 partner. Especially in finances, when this type of thinking enters a relationship, things can easily start to fall apart. When women are forced to contribute more than they are comfortable with, they begin to become slightly vindictive in their everyday dealing with their families. These things go unnoticed by the man. He thinks that things are going just great. The woman begins to talk with her best friends and her mother about things that are taking place in her marriage. These accusations on behalf of the wife start slow and heat up as time goes on. Women are not in complete agreement with the way the family dynamics are going, but they may not say they are not pleased. She tends to agree with the man to keep peace within the home and for fear of disapproval. This indicates that the two humans, the man and the woman, have totally different dynamics in their way of thinking and looking at a situation.

Men must remember that the only way to enter this earth is through the womb of a woman. Men, when you get married, you have in essence just married your mother only in a different way of life. Your wife seeks a closeness that is seemingly hard for men to always understand. When you have just left your wife for less than thirty minutes and she calls you and says that she is lonesome, what do men do? He is out with the boys for poker night, and golf day among other things.

Men, remember you are not a woman. Men, why can't you understand? How do you react when she wants a day out? When you pull out of the driveway at home and your phone rings? It is your wife and you reply, "What do you want now!" Men, you should say, "I miss you dear, is there something I can pick up for you on my return trip home?" You might find, men, that your wife will be shocked by your response and she may even forget what she called you for.

A woman's mind is continually running twenty-four-seven. A woman's mind stays in gear while men are asleep. Always remember, men, that God had you in mind when He made woman from Adam's and your rib. God knew that men would need a "help meet." Most men need a little help in getting all of his things together. Husbands and wives should always complement each other. The woman has already started the day when the man is still asleep. She is also most often the last to go to bed as she has kids, clothes, dishes and other things to prepare for the next day. She completes the man.

Men, why not honor her instead of taking her for granted. If this is not you, my man, you have my thanks. Pass this book to your friend who treats his wife or fiance this way. Join me in spreading the word rather than being defensive. Help me to honor the woman who has given us life.

CHAPTER SIX

Who Do You Think You Are?

Remember, Christian men, one day you will have to answer for the deeds that were done on earth. One of the things that is going to haunt you is your treatment of God's woman. Check my grammar, I said "God's woman." That will be the day that you will finally realize that you did not own anything in this world. It may be too late so I urge you to wake up! In dealing with the things in life based on the way society is structured, you will always have problems trying to change things. The powerful and the privileged are the people who are setting the standard. This is not equal to saying that, "All is correct." Most people are of the understanding that when the majority of society is doing something it must be correct. This statement is not entirely true.

One of the things that comes to mind is the struggle that women have undergone in the entire world. The hardships that women have endured from the beginning of time have been accepted by the majority of the people. Society has accepted this treatment. Society and the majority have acted in a very displeasing and unacceptable manner. One would think that after all of the media attention and all of these higher learning institutions, Bible teaching Ministries and various other things that show that women are the same as men, our ideas about women would change.

The most notable difference between the sexes is that "She is a woman and he is a man." Now that all of the readers understand what is being dealt with I will move on. Man, throughout his years on this planet, has not fully understood the facts of life as it relates to the woman. The woman is a person. She is the same person with ideas and opinions as the man. She has a mind and she is capable of thinking. She has been blessed with certain gifts that are and have been very badly damaged through the years due to man's stubborn nature. Man has been dominating women since the beginning of time, and this has caused the woman to accept this position in society. When things are structured a certain way for a long period of time the people involved begin to think that things are okay. You always hear people say things like, "It has been this way forever." This makes me believe that these people are ignorant of the fact that things can be changed.

Let's take a look at who women are in this world today. I would say that women are living under false pretense. They have always followed the leader. They have never in their entire lives taken the time to find out who they really are. They were not designed to be treated or put in the position that they now enjoy. They were and have been led in this direction by the Leader. The Leader has been leading them into positions that are not places that men will respect or think of treating them as being equal to him.

I will define the meaning of the word "Leader" for you. A Leader is one who decides the manner and direction in which things should be decided upon and the way in which things should go. The Leader is the type of man Adam was to be as designed by God. However, the woman has allowed the Leader to portray her as being nothing more than a sex symbol. This style of life for women has contributed greatly to women not attaining equal status in the workplace. Women have allowed men to set up prostitute houses as well. All of these things were initially started by men.

This word Leader needs to be put in front of man. The reason is he does not and has not fully understood the real meaning of the word. A Leader has been established so that things are kept in order. The Leader is supposed to protect. He is responsible for the direction in which he is leading his followers. He is not supposed to solicit or exploit the people that he is leading, and he is supposed to be leading women instead of visiting them in the prostitute houses. How can you consider yourself a leader when you are helping to exploit the ones you are leading? Men are supposed to be leading; men have the ability to lead. Men have continued to portray themselves as being the leading man.

Now, it is time for the woman to emerge with the determination to inform the man that he must live up to the job he has been selected for since the beginning of creation. The woman has the being to present to him the things he should have been doing down through the years of his leadership. He has been doing things which are very apparent to the world that have become traditional rather than doing what is right. There are a large number of men that know that man has been leading the women into things that are very degrading to the woman however they do not speak up as leaders either. Therefore, this also contributes to the continuing treatment of the woman as though she is not equal to man.

I believe that most of the people who may read this book have heard the saying, "This is a man's world." This saying is partially true; this world as we know it to be today could not continue without the woman. I have yet to see a man give birth, therefore it should be said that this is a man's and woman's world. The people in the world who are considered leaders are the ones who are mostly responsible for the problems between men and women.

Men, for some unknown reason, have forgotten that they were put on earth as leaders. If one takes a very good look at the way women have been held to a standard, that is considered okay with men. The various religious leaders seem to be in agreement with the unequal treatment of women as well. Man seems to equate leadership with being superior. This is where it all started. The believer and the non-believer in this world could be leaning to this type of understanding. There is no reason for any man on the planet to come to this conclusion because every man who has entered this earth's realm came because of the woman. This being the universal standard, you would think that all men would see themselves for what they really are—they are human beings just as the woman. They are both human beings.

Most people who are not Christians do not understand the Scripture when it states, "We suffer for a lack of knowledge" (Hosea 4:6). The man is suffering everyday for or because of his lack of knowledge. Man was designed to always keep things in order in the earth's realm. If the woman strayed in an unreasonable way, he is to reel her in but not try to dominate her because he is physically stronger than the woman. Man was not given extra strength to dominate women. His strength has been given to him to protect her, to treat her as though she were weaker than him. This kind of treatment was designed by God?not by man.

Man is supposed to look at creation from God's perspective—not from man's perspective. When man creates his own world then he will be allowed to use his own ideas. Presently, this is not the situation. He is to treat the woman by divine principles. This is the only way we will ever have peace on earth.

In order for one to be a true leader, he must possess certain qualities. He needs to read and study the definition of a leader and the definition of domination. According to man's mentality, he has gotten the understanding of the two words very wrong. He thinks that domination is leadership. He dominates the woman, yet, he is the one you see on TV using women at an alarming rate. Men are getting women to get telephone service for them, buy cars for them, and allow them to use their credit worthiness, use their apartments and houses, and to bond them out of jail. Men, I ask, "Who do you think you are?" Men are not using the qualities that define them as being either a man or a leader. This situation has really gotten bad in the last ten years. Men, who are supposed to be leaders, have been incarcerated at above normal rates and, surprisingly, women seem to love prison inmates.

If you have the opportunity to visit a foreign country and observe the special treatment that men offer to women of a different ethnic group you will also understand the differences between men and women. The women respond very graciously in foreign countries to the treatment of their men. This would indicate that women would like this special treatment. I am amazed to find or notice this situation going on in places that I have visited. I have visited many, many countries and I have encountered nearly all ethnic groups in several of the countries I have visited.

For example, when I visited the market in Italy, I saw many women carrying very heavy bags. I believe the Italian man should be carrying these bags, not because she can't carry the bags but because God design the system the other way around. Men should assist the woman in carrying heavy bags but in Italy I observed that, even though the man may have accompanied the woman, he does not offer to carry her heavy bags." The custom being, I am told, is that the women go each day to get food for lunch and dinner and this is their role. Where are the men? Having a caffe? Men, to this I will add, when you see your wife or mother at the door with heavy bags in their arms or hands you should stop whatever you are doing and go assist them. This type of treatment I observed at the Italian Market has gone on far too long, so even women feel that this would have to be God's order of things. The feelings of being slightly inferior have become common place in most societies among women. The women in countries outside of the United States are much worse off than the American woman. Also, I observed in places where the economy is very bad, the situation is even worse. The main reason for this type of problem being greater in the poorer countries is because the man is the main bread winner. This means that the woman is totally dependent on him for her and her family's survival. This partially explains why women have come to accept this type of treatment in their respective countries.

I also would like to note that in this inferior treatment of women, the man likes to feel that he has full control of his wife and that he is able to do almost anything he chooses. He can slap her around, have several other relationships, stay out as late as he wants, and the list of mistreatment goes on and on. This behavior has to stop. The woman must finally stand up for her rights and self worth. She must be made aware of the fact that God did not design the system to work like that. She must come into the understanding that there are ways of a man that seem right to him, but they are not right in accordance with how God intended man and woman to live together. This way of thinking or feeling has nothing to do with the way that God designed the system to work between a man and a woman. God made a very different design when he made woman.

The first thing to look at in this situation is the fact that God, who created human life, did not make one human superior or inferior to the other. It is stated that, "We were all created equal." This would surely indicate that God created the woman especially for the man, and since He gave her the ability to give birth to man, it should indicate to all sensible people that since man has to enter the earth realm through the womb of a woman, he could not therefore be possibly superior to her. The woman is the reason for man's entrance upon the earth and all life enters through the woman. How it is that man has not fully understood this? In all of these years, from the beginning of time, man has not fully understood God's order. When the order of mankind was established at the beginning, man misunderstood.

You must take into consideration that when God does things, He does them decently and in order. Also, one of the biblical principles is that the things that He has established should be kept in the exact order that He established them. From the beginning of time until this present day, the only way human life enters planet earth is through the woman. This fully indicates that one must be very careful before tampering with what God has established. God had a very good reason for giving man a help meet. God knows man's heart. He also knows the needs of man. Man will quickly say that these things are not exactly what he needs, especially a woman, yet most men are womanizers. This is one of the reasons why there is so much distrust between women and men.

This goes into marriage as I have stated before: "Woman enjoy the state of their existence in this society." They enjoy this because they have not taken the time to research the Bible teachings relative to the way that God designed women. Women have, for the most part, aligned their lives based on history. History should not be fully accepted. The Bible should be in the forefront of the total assessment of how life should be lived. This scenario, when put into play, would show how women have been mistreated for centuries. Men, who do you think you are? I always come back to that question because a man is born of a woman. Then this other question comes to mind: "What is the problem?" The problem is that man is determined to be a dominator of women. It is much easier to be a dominator than it is to be a leader.

CHAPTER SEVEN

You Will Ascend in the New Year

The year of Jubilee denotes change. The changes in the Bible come from the spiritual realm into the physical realm. When the physical realm fully realizes what the spiritual realm is doing, then it can easily be achieved. First things first—in order to grasp things from the spiritual realm you must be in the order that God has designed. God made the woman in His image and likeness. Are you or have you remained in His image and likeness according to His Word? Have you let man exploit you and change you into believing that you are a sex symbol? Remember the Scripture says, "Give unto Caesar what is his and give unto God what is His."

With this in mind the things that have had the most profound effect on women have been men. The woman has taken this to the level that is unacceptable to God. The Bible states that, "The man is to be the Leader." The Bible did not say that the man was to be the leader of the woman in the absence of God. My Bible states that when you are choosing things relative to the Scriptures, "One should choose wisely." This is the year that the woman must choose wisely. When you choose God you cannot be wrong. God is a jealous God.

I have a feeling that a very large number of women who are reading the Bible daily have failed to realize that they have let go of something that is a basic principle of life as well. God has given you everything you need to fully accomplish your goal. First, you must redefine who you are in Christ, then you must get back in order with God. This information is enough to take you higher in 2012. This information is written to elevate your thinking. You will never rise above your thinking. Realize that you are where you are today because your thinking was not in its proper order. This situation runs far deeper than I first envisioned it to be.

Women far out-number men in life; with the larger number of men being killed in wars and being incarcerated this makes the number of women even larger. You would think that this would bring the status of women to another level; however, men still remain in the higher places. Usually, this would be a greater chance of bringing things into proper order. I have taken quite some time to look into why the process has taken all of these years with such slow progress. The main problem is the infighting among women. Women have an unnoticed problem; women have other women as their problem as well. Women, for the most part, are looking at other women as their problem. The woman's problem is with the man, the one they are following. Never take your eyes off the leader you are following. Leaders are very slow in processing things relative to women because they know and recognize the continuous infighting among women. Instead of women concentrating their efforts directly on the problem, they are focused in other directions.

However, the year of 2012 should be the year that all women are released from the lies that have been written about them. The cruelty toward women was started by man. The unequal treatment was started by man. The beatings were started by man. The houses of ill repute were started by man. The constitution was written by men that were born of a woman. I know that this information is startling. The women that fought for their right to vote had war waged against them by their sons, the very sons whom they had given birth to and brought into the earth realm. Maybe in Book 2, I will explain to women how to properly address this situation. There are many Bible verses that have been misrepresented in a manner that makes the situation relative to a woman being equal to man impossible to be understood. These kinds of things have gone on far too long. Now is the time for the woman to recognize that things need to be changed.

Men have used the kindness of women, including their mothers, to continue this type of behavior which is contrary to the design of a woman. The woman was designed to be cherished, honored, adored, and be appreciated for having accepted the part whereby all humans enter into the world. She has a dual assignment—to give birth to both male and female babies. Anyone who then thinks that she could possibly be less than a man should have their brains examined. You read about people being admitted to the mental institutions, sometimes I think they have admitted the wrong people.

I cannot fathom the thought or idea that my mother could have been considered less than the son that she conceived in her womb. In fact, when I think about my mother I have more respect and honor for her than one could imagine. My mother was a godly woman who always addressed me in a manner with statements that showed she understood the problems that women faced relative to the way they were being treated. She was trying to elevate my thinking to a higher level in respect to the treatment of women. So, for me to exploit the woman, was my own doing, because I understood how to treat a woman I had the learning or the technical know how but I had the ungodly spirits I had to get rid of before I could understand exactly how I should treat women.

However, some men do not recognize that the ungodly spirits are operating in their lives. Everything that has been organized to further remove the woman from her proper position is finally coming to light in this year. The cover is being removed. The real truth is beginning to emerge. Some of the man's practices have gone unnoticed for years and years. No one person has been willing to step up to the plate and do what is supposed to be done; it takes a special type of individual to connect the dots to get this design on the proper path. I will introduce you to one person who is all for putting things in God's order and that person is me.

I grew up in a Christian environment. I was a trustee

in the Church and a baptized believer who was married. However, I did not operate in the principles of God until I began to study the Bible. In so doing, I was able to then define exactly what was written in the Bible for me as a man and for any man who will take the time to study the Bible and to apply it to his life as well. From my studies I learned God's order of things. Now I am able to share what I learned with women and men and to open their eyes to the situations that have hindered women in their past which will more than likely hinder them in their future as well.

The answer to the problem is in recognizing who has set the order and then make immediate changes. You must keep in mind at all times that the Bible states that, "You will suffer for a lack of knowledge." I am hoping that every woman that reads this book will ask the question, "What can we do because of Jesus?" I would hope that from this book the women would begin to follow the principles of Jesus and not the principles of man unless the principles of man are in order with God. Although 2012 is your year to ascend, women, you must remain remarkably sober and not become dramatic and always suppress the urge to think of yourselves more highly than you ought to. You have for all of your lives had your eyes on man. Now is the time for you to take a look at what made all of this possible.

Remember, the Bible states, you can do all things through Christ who strengthens you (Philippians 4:13). This can help you to jump start things in 2012. I have written this book so that you may identify your life's real purpose. So to the woman I say, I hope you get new insight and come closer to finding and discovering who you really are! In your excitement to get access to even more life changing information, always remember that you are receiving this because it is time for you to ascend higher in 2012. The time has arrived for a vast change in the thinking process of the men in the world when it relates to the woman. The woman has endured this unequal treatment for ages. Armed with the information in this book, women will be able to move quickly into the mainstream of being the woman that God created them to be.

The woman was given a special assignment when she was formed. She has done most of it. In keeping with her assignment, she has sort of strayed into being led the wrong way by the man. She, being the kind-hearted and trusting woman that she is, has moved herself from the values that should have been kept. Instead of following and keeping the values that were bestowed on her by God, she moved away from them. Some of these values which God bestowed upon the woman are very precious in that she was given the understanding of how to care for children; that is, how to become a mother. She was given the ability to take care of several things at one time; she is a multi-tasker in today's society.

Women are simply more unique than men. For instance, my wife has seven senses, yes, that's seven senses, while I have only six. God gave her something that I don't have. I recognize this in all women, and that is their sensory perception is much greater than that of the average man. Now, with these things in mind, the women should understand the reason I have for sharing this information. One reason is because I am bursting with excitement to share this with you. I am positive that this book will be an inspiration to womankind. I should have let the cat out of the bag before now. I am not a person who likes to write. I have given the information contained in this book careful thought for several years before attempting to write this book. And I am willing to sacrifice my dislike of writing to provide you with this valuable information. Now that I have a wealth of information I will be able to answer questions of whoever asks. The ascending higher position for women has been far too long in coming. The time is now! Women, it is your time to close the gap!

This gap which I am addressing is the mistaken identity of women. The woman has not been identified in her proper attributes, abilities, order, and perspective. She has much more to offer than is projected in that she has not been given a full opportunity to express or show that she can do many things. When you finish reading this book you will have a handle on how and why it is necessary at this time. There is a time and a season for everything.

Women, 2012 is your season to ascend. There is a time and a season for things to remain the same. This is the season for the woman to come into her full potential. The woman has been a survivor; she has endured all of the unnecessary obstacles that women are faced with daily. One such problem that women face is on the job, and that is women are constantly under pressure when they are dealing with men in the workplace. I am not saying that all men treat women unfairly, but what I am saying is that men have the mindset that women are not their equal. Men that are married usually have the same mind set as well. Men are usually closer to their mothers, and since men are closer to their mothers you would think that some day he would wake up and realize that his wife is a mother as well. As a man, I cannot understand how this kind of thinking could be in existence. We are living in one of the greatest countries in the entire world. With all of this country's greatness, we as a people of higher learning and a nation of various religious teachings, with most men associated with political, judicial, and business organizations, are still living in the dark ages when it comes to understanding who God made the woman to be. The negative things that women endure because they are women need to end. The season and the time is now. Women, you will ascend in 2012! You will be fully pleased with your accomplishments in the coming years. I believe that this transformation will move very quickly when the woman fully understands God's order. I am not talking about man's order. My reason for making this statement at this time is for the women to look past man for a moment. Notice what I did not say. I did not say, "Look past man permanently." The woman and man have to perform in the position that was designed by God during the creation. Women, during your evaluations, please keep in mind that you are still a child of the King, and that is King Jesus.

The question is, "Who will you trust?" Women, you have been trusting man instead of God. Your focus is out of God's order. Regardless of what happened in the past you must take the first step. The first step is to turn to the things of God. The Bible is to be used as a guide. You have not followed the Biblical teachings. You have followed the world's teachings. You have allowed yourselves to be used and be seen mainly as a sex symbol. When this situation is reversed you will have moved into the place that God designed for you and that God has allowed you to be in because God will allow you to be the woman that you are. Women, you are operating out of God's design. The way you operate now is not how you were designed to be. If you dwell on the people that have caused things to be out of God's order instead of focusing on God you will wake up tomorrow without the help of God.

With God on our side you will ascend higher in 2012. It is impossible to fail when God is on your side. The magnitude of the situation that women are presently encountering is this: women are being accepted in many, many higher positions in government and also in the private sector. Notice that I did not say "all sectors." The woman has been slowly included because of the stigma that has been placed on her by the men. The men have been doing this type of thing for centuries. When a situation has been allowed to be in progress for centuries you must deal with it in a very different way. There are ways that this can be dealt with. The way that women are dealing with this will not solve this situation in many, many years to come. They are and have been making progress however at the rate of their progress it will take more than two hundred years to get ahead.

Looking at the numbers, women should realize that a change is necessary to achieve their goal. Women are trying so desperately to achieve their goal, but women I say to you, it's not a goal, it's a birthright. The first day of your life on earth you ultimately had achieved the goal that you feel is necessary. You are fighting a battle that will take more time to be achieved by the women reading this book.

Think about what is written in this book. This book shows you some of the things that you are doing wrong. You have been in this situation since birth. Your mothers accepted it for their entire lifetime. Now let's deal with the statement in another paragraph. I alluded to the fact that being a leader does not equate to ownership. The women in the free world act as though they were owned by the leaders. The movie industry, prostitution, marriage, the church, billboard industry, strip club industry, and the magazine industry are all agencies designed to degrade women without their full knowledge of what the leader is doing to or for the woman.

Notice how many times I use the word design. I want all of the women that read this book to study the word design. The word design takes on a special meaning. You are God's design. Think about it. You were especially designed to be a woman. Never let anyone take your design from you. Remember that man was created first. Then God designed you especially to be a help meet to the man. Never let anyone or anything distract you from your original design. Look in the mirror and take a look at yourself with the utmost appreciation for your special design. Stop letting men dominate you.

Men are to be leaders. When you discover that he is out of the order of God then you as a woman should remind him of the fact that he is supposed to lead you and protect you at all times. When women begin to exercise their design and begin to show the men that they are very special this will hopefully encourage men to appreciate them for who they really are. The treatment of men towards the woman was never intended to be as it is portrayed around the world today. When you consider how other religions treat women in America it really is unbelievable. This type of wake up information as to the real value of a woman holds men to a much higher expectation of who the woman really is and how they should be treated. After reading this book, I am confident that you will stop making excuses. You have to start making decisions based on Biblical teachings.

Women, get up and go to someone that fully understands the Bible teaching. In addition, go and sit around them. Don't make any excuses as to why you cannot make the necessary changes to become a godly woman and not just a sex symbol. Women, you have strong characters and you are free to make decisions that are relative to a closer walk with the Creator. This can be achieved if you believe that God will make good on His promises. God never breaks His promises. We are the ones that sometimes break promises. Women, based on using the information in this book you will understand that the ideal time is right now! Nothing else will do! You must bring forth that inner power that God put in you. The power to ascend only needs to be released. There is more in doing this than you will ever understand until it has been done.

As I stated before, you have all of the qualifications to get it finished. You will be doing the right thing at the right time and for the right reasons. I can say for a fact that women are far more intelligent than men usually give them credit for. I see this situation as being a very short journey for the woman to make. If women will make the necessary changes they find in this book, then their journey to making those changes a reality will be easier to achieve. Women, you are coming to realize that when Jesus made the statement on the cross that, "It is finished," this indicated that everything that you will ever need is finished in the spiritual realm. Now you need only to understand from the written Word how to bring it into this physical world. It is easy only if it is done in God's order, otherwise you will have a much longer journey ahead of you.

The race to ascend is not just to the swift but to he or she that endureth to the end. In order to endure you must first have understood why women have not obtained equality. First, women need to be considered as an equal to the man. I have not been able as of this date to find anything written in the Bible that would lead man to thinking the way he does about women. For most of my life, the statement, "this is a man's world" has been echoed. It has been incorrectly stated for years and years. It should have been stated this way: "This is a man's and woman's world."

I want all women to go back and read my last statement again. Notice what I said, "Any man in his right mind knows that this world is both a man's and woman's world." I have addressed several things that the woman should always consider when she is dealing with the average man. The man for the most part of his life wants to feel superior to his woman or to women in general. Some women are talking with men in small groups when the man will make statements that will degrade women. Then he will turn to the woman in the group and say, "I was only kidding," and try to make a joke of the incident. I am letting it be known here and now that he is and was not kidding. These kind of foul statements about women are in almost all of the men's conversation relative to women. Women should always be alert when you walk in and men begin to laugh. It's because someone has noticed the entering of a woman and had changed the subject.

Let me share this with you: while sitting with other men, we are usually talking and discussing our relationship problems that men are having with their wives. One of them would gesture with his hands and say, "That woman!" One man recounted this: "I came home and the girl was checking my shirt pockets for notes and going through my numbers in the check book, etc." These are the kinds of things men discuss in groups or with other men. Saying things like, "She is worrying me about paying that bill because she thinks I spent the money on something else. She asked what happen to all the money that I have." Another may add, "That woman is always on me about money! Man, I just don't know what is wrong with those women." These types of questions and statements surface during many men's conversations. Many men cannot ride from home to church without getting into an argument with their wives.

Women, you must know that you are usually the main subject of most men's conversation and you may be in the same conversational category as sports. This, in itself, should give you some idea of what I am alluding to in this book of explanations about men's behavior. I am by no means stating that women are not talking about men. I am saying that men, as a whole, continue to make degrading statements about women. When these statements are made, the men look at the man as being okay and the woman as being loose. This type of understanding should have been addressed directly years and years ago. This change has been left on the back burner too long. I will at some point push the women in the right direction to accomplish what is really rightfully hers. Equality and full acceptance is the next step. Your desire is to accumulate more power. Women, you do not need more power. You only need to turn to the principles of God. You do not realize that you have rejected the teachings of the Bible. Women have been too focused on the man more than they have been focused on God's teachings. The woman has not fully understood that she has rejected the teachings of the Bible. My Bible states that, "God is a jealous God." This would equate to the level that you, the woman, cannot place man in front of God and His teachings. I hope that the words in this book will not fall on deaf ears.

I repeat again that God is a God of order. Women have allowed man to lead them in many wrong directions. Presently, the woman has been led so far from the order of God that she doesn't recognize that she is out of order. Now is the appointed time to take a serious look at the message according to the word of God. According to the Bible that I read, the Word of God states that, 'His Word would last.' Women, wake up and move into God's divine order. The order that is stated in the Bible has been far too long ignored. The Bible states that the women should obey their husbands. This statement has been taken out of context. The other statement that is being misunderstood is that the woman should honor her husband. This is a correct statement. Men are commanded by God to honor their wives. The Bible verses are very clear. These statements are written so that they apply to both the man and the woman.

For instance, when a couple is getting married they both are supposed to respect and honor each other. The only way we can bring balance into the marriage is if both of them respect and honor each other. The man seems to forget that the woman was made from him. The next thing that both men and women forget is that, "When you are married you become one."

Without the understanding of obedience, you have been kept from crossing the mountains and now you have allowed yourselves to stumble over the pebbles of life. This scenario is mind boggling to the man that is writing this book. I am hoping that the women who are reading this book will try to understand its content as you realize that it's written to elevate your thinking. You must always think of yourself as a winner. You have been working on the symptoms for years and years. Now the time has come to go to the source and correct the problem. You have been misled by the very one that was conceived by you. I hope that this information will shock women into ingesting this book. This book is invaluable information which will vault you to your proper place that God designed for you to be in.

Remember not to take this information out of context. First, you must adhere to order. Remember always that God is a God of order. This statement somehow seems to baffle some women. One of the main reasons women have not received full recognition is because they have not adhered to God's order. In this world, you read in the newspaper about the world's order. In this book, I am writing about and addressing God's order. If you have not fully understood the differences between the world's order and God's order you will have difficulty understanding what is written in this book. There are obstacles in all paths of life. In order to by-pass the obstacles you must first adhere to the order. That word order carries a lot of insight into the way things are achieved. Without the proper order, you will stumble over the pebbles. This should not be, because you have the written Word to follow. Women and men are not following the written Word. The Word can be your greatest friend or your greatest enemy. I am your greatest helper. I will push you to no longer accepting this unequal situation that has been tolerated by society. The Biblical scholar in the workplace and the governments of the entire world have a problem with this. The women in this world have not quite figured out how to address this in a manner to get it quickly resolved. However, I am considering the possibility of telling the woman or showing them how to speed up the process. The reason that the process has moved so slow through the years is because the woman has been living according to man's thinking rather than by God's design for her.

This book is written to address exactly who the woman is. She has been attacked on all fronts of life. The things that women are being attacked for are totally insane. Yet, she has maintained her sanity, pride, and dignity as she goes forth proclaiming God's gift to her based on biblical principles of God's design of a woman.

About the Author

James R. Mitchell is well known as a man of God who always has a message for anyone who will listen. He is not afraid to talk to those who struggle with listening to or receiving his message. Well known as "Mr. Mitch," he saw the need to heed his dream to help men understand women. This book offers a message of teaching, guidance, and courage for men to understand the "Design of a Woman."

Teaching men to recognize, honor, and respect God's creature who brings forth all human creation needs to be a priority in today's society. This book is written as a testimony of the knowledge James Mitchell has gained in his 76 years of observing, living with, honoring, and now through God's Word, having an appreciation and deep understanding of the unique design of a woman. James Mitchell says, "many mistakes were made by myself as well, when it came to women, but through the years, by the grace of God, I found my soul-mate and I have learned that knowing a woman is now uppermost if you are to love her as God created her. "Design of a Woman" is written from my perspective on a woman and how she should be treated, as it provides a self-help guide to help men and women love and nurture the unique bond and love the two can have."

Mr. Mitch provides Biblical knowledge and wisdom to clarify his godly vision which is unique to the design of a blessed, virtuous woman and how man can learn how to treat that help meet God has blessed him with. His mission is to assist those who suffer for a lack of knowledge regarding the design of a woman.

Author's Note

Most of the information that I have included in this book came from thousands of emails and conversations of friends and relatives. Some information is drawn from my personal experience, private conversations with singles, married couples and my sons and daughters.

The other information comes from my extensive study of the Bible. I have listened to many preachers, teachers, and Biblical scholars. Yet, most of them do not consider their wives as equals. When talking to most men regardless of their position in life they rarely say, "My wife is my equal." Instead I hear many men say, "My wife and I have different responsibilities." I have not accepted man's logic relative to the woman, neither have I found his logic in the Word of God, only in the word of man. Whose report are you going to believe? This statement is for all of the "Legal Christians" and also for people that understand the "Truth."

Reviews

I am finishing the Design of a Woman as I travel from Naples, Italy to Marrakech, Morocco (Africa). I enjoyed reading this book because it is written for both men and women. The thoughts and ideas will not be easily digested by men and women, who have not studied the Bible, but they will be exposed to the message and the seed will be planted. I found this book to be eye opening because at the moment, as I am traveling to Africa, I am delayed in Brussels, Belgium in October. It is cold, and I am without a coat, "It's not cold in Africa." Women are truly uniquely designed and are created by God to love and to be loved, appreciated, honored and supported. Brother Mitch captures this from a Biblical aspect in his book, The Design of a Woman.

I would have enjoyed scriptures being included as references throughout the book. I am familiar with a lot of the biblical truths referenced, but to someone who is being exposed to this for the first time it may be overwhelming and they may feel under qualified to start searching the Bible for such truths. I would have also enjoyed reading about the women that are walking in

God's order and the men that would lay down their lives for their wives and family.

The Design of a Woman includes advice from Mr. Mitch from a father's perspective to men and women. He covers sensitive topics on how we should be leaders and not dominators, how women should present themselves and how men should support and treat women as their equal. He shares his life experiences and observations of how a man and woman should share the same positions within God's Ordained Order.

I like this book because it is targeting all men and women. Mr. Mitch has a call to action echoed throughout his book. He has identified, through his research and life experiences, a deep seeded deficiency in the way we relate to one another according to God's divine Order. This book is excellent for the woman who may not fully understand how much God loved her when He created her. This book is a must for the man who has never considered or appreciated how fearfully and wonderfully God has designed the women in our lives.

Minister Ronald L. Freeman Jr.
Naples, Italy

I would like to thank Mr. Mitch for giving me the opportunity to read and review his outstanding book written to the men and women of today. In reading this book, I have come to understand the greatest thing about the creation of man and woman and that is, men and women were created by God to live in harmony and love with each other. Mr. Mitch has used relevant life situations and examples as well as sound Biblical principles to shed light on a situation that may have been puzzling to most of us for a very long time. I would recommend the reading of this enlightening book to both men and women for in it they will find the very foundations of what it means to walk in the Divine Order in which God intended man and woman to walk in and live in as well.

I truly thank Mr. Mitch for bringing to the forefront this situation between men and women and using his vast experience and research to help us understand God's Divine Order for our lives as men and women. I would say to the reader to take their time and read this book prayerfully, and with an intended purpose to finish this book with an understanding and enlightenment that they can change their lives to live according to God's great design for women and men.

Minister Alfredia R. DeVita
Naples, Italy